In The Ring

Orienthia Speakman

International Standard Book Number 13: 978-1948731058
Cover Design by Dream Design Graphics

Editing provided by Publish*her* Publishing

www.publishher.org

IN THE RING

DEDICATION

We dedicate this devotional to our FAB 5 plus 1!

Vincent Jr., Quovadia, Ebony, Alexcia (Miguel our future "sonNlove"), and Creston Joshua. As parents, our hope has always been that each of you learn from our mistakes and our successes as a married couple. We've modeled some tough times in our marriage in front of you guys, yet, we wouldn't change a thing. Part of the reason Vincent and I have fought so hard for a healthy marriage, even when it was so easy to throw in the towel, is because we wanted you all to see the power of God through our love for each other.

We truly appreciate the love and support that each of you have brought into our lives, and to be parents of all of you is such a pleasure. Our prayer is that our blended family will continue to thrive and grow closer as we all continue to grow in Christ! We love you all immensely! .

INTRODUCTION

Imagine having the perfect marriage, now pinch yourself because the reality is, it doesn't exist! Marriages are composed of two people, from diverse backgrounds, striving to be ONE. As if that thought isn't hard enough, we compound the issue with thoughts of perfection, which end up putting us in an ongoing fight. My husband and I discovered this fact as our marriage seemed to go off the cliff for two years as we were headed for divorce! Through the help of God and our willingness to learn to fight for each other instead of against one another, we restored our union.

This 31-day devotional and workbook was written to help couples learn to fight together instead of being on opposite ends of the ring. As you and your spouse take a moment to read through each day, our prayer is that your heart is open to hearing the Holy Spirit minister to the both of you concerning the areas discussed. Our hope is that you learn to get into the ring together and fight for what's yours, a healthy marriage. Each day, there is a quote and/or Scripture reference for meditation, my husband's or my thoughts on it, a challenge for the both of you, and a prayer to assist with enhancing your relationship.

There are 10 subject matters that we discuss in our unique way. These were key issues in our marriage that seemed to keep us on opposite ends of the ring. We wanted to add a little humor to our insight, praying that it will bring you both closer together in your union. Using boxing terms was our idea to encourage you to fight together. Keep in mind that these are our opinions and areas that we felt would be helpful to marriages. Listed below is a summary of what each of those subject matters represents:

GO THE DISTANCE: Our communication is able to go the distance or create distance. The mouth and how it can make or break your marriage is the focus of this topic.

ROLL WITH THE PUNCHES: Nobody wants to take a hit to their wants and/or desires. In every marriage, there are tasks that neither one of you wants to do as a couple, yet you know it must be done. This subject focuses on challenging us to go with the flow in order to maintain peace in our relationship.

HITTING BELOW THE BELT: Any notable spouse knows his or her partner's weakness. Using those weakness to hurt or harm the marriage is a no go and is considered hitting below the belt. We all have actions or responses that we know we shouldn't have toward our spouse, but we do anyway. This opens our eyes and brings the accountability factor mentioned in *Marriage Vs Ministry: The Fight Of My Life.*

MAIN EVENT: This subject concerns intimacy and SEX in your Marriage. Need I say more? No one wants to miss the main event. This is an almost forbidden topic in the church, but it's also one of THE MOST NEEDED FACTORS IN YOUR MARRIAGE. We will address this!

THE PURSE: In boxing, there is a goal: to win the purse. Many fights happen over money. This addresses financial issues that couples usually go many rounds about.

These next two don't really have a meaning connected to boxing, but my Chocolate Drop is such a man of wisdom that I had to share his thoughts. I also added the Caramel Princess because we didn't want to leave anyone out.

CHOCOLATE DROP MOMENTS: Just a few concerns my husband believes most men want to tell their wives without offending them.

CARAMEL PRINCESS MOMENTS: Just a few topics that I wanted to share with the husbands without them feeling overwhelmed.

PUT SOME RESPECT ON IT: Disrespect has caused more than enough fights. It is able to sneak in through the attitude of the heart. We want to challenge ways that couples honor their spouses.

SAVED BY THE BELL: The bell weighs in on your situation. Sometimes, you are carrying too much or doing too much in an area that is making other areas deficient. Balancing your marriage as you incorporate family, children, ministry, and business truly brings salvation to your marriage.

COMBINATION: There are times when areas in your marriage will require a "one, two, punch." You have to combine your efforts to produce what you want, which is more.

DAY ONE

GO THE DISTANCE

"A nagging spouse is like the drip, drip, drip of a leaky faucet; You can't turn it off, and you can't get away from it."

Proverbs 27:15-16 (MSG)

My Thoughts: Complaining, grumbling and fault-finding towards your spouse is not going to motivate him or her to do better. It only aggravates the situation and usually causes your spouse to go in the opposite direction of your request. Nagging your spouse pushes him or her further away from you and creates division in your household. Nagging reflects frustration, negative emotions, and often disappointment. This is usually hurtful to your spouse as the recipient and could cause him or her to retaliate. Nagging not only affects your spouse but exposes emotions that you (the nagger) have not properly dealt with within. Those negative emotions that cause you to become fussy will soon become explosives that will result in collateral damage in your relationship. Keep in mind nagging doesn't make you right; it just makes everyone angry and uncomfortable!

CHALLENGE: Practice using a calming tone when making a request. Instead of using the words "You need to" or "You better," try "Honey, will you…" or "Babe, please don't forget..." Be sure to focus on showing appreciation more than correction. A positive attitude when addressing an issue usually comes out better than a negative presentation. On the flip side, take time out to deal with the emotions within you that make you the nagger. Ask yourself, "Am I really angry about what I'm nagging about, or is it just my way of showing my disappointment about something else?" Talk it out with your spouse or a third party before discord settles into your relationship.

PRAYER: Lord, please help me to be a soothing fountain and not a leaking faucet in my marriage. Provide me the wisdom to use the appropriate words that will motivate my spouse instead of aggravate. Make my tone soothing to my spouse's ears and pleasant to my spouse's heart. Lord, use my words to heal instead of hurt.

IN THE RING

DAY 2

ROLL WITH THE PUNCHES

"Admit your faults to one another and pray for each other so that you may be healed. The earnest prayer of a righteous man has great power and wonderful results."

James 5:16

My Thoughts: Apologizing, for many of us, feels like a household chore. Nobody wants to do it, but it must be done. Admitting you are wrong or have been offensive to your spouse is the best route. Apologizing quickly and effectively can keep the devil from making little issues become disastrous. Offering an apology simply means that my spouse's feelings are way more important than me being right. A sincere apology is a pathway to reconciliation, which means now you get to make up (if you know what I mean)!

CHALLENGE: Practice apologizing quickly when you recognize you have been offensive or have hurt your mate. Acknowledge your wrong, ask for forgiveness, and be willing to back up your words with a change in your action. This way, your "I'm sorry" is viewed as sincere.

PRAYER: *Father, show us areas where we have hurt each other. Give us the heart and mind to apologize quickly and effectively to each other. Lord, we don't want our prayers to be hindered. Help us both to realize that apologizing is necessary to keep our spiritual houses clean.*

DAY 3

HITTING BELOW THE BELT

"Don't pick on people, jump on their failures, criticize their faults—unless, of course, you want the same treatment. Don't condemn those who are down; that hardness can boomerang. Be easy on people; you'll find life a lot easier. Give away your life; you'll find life given back, but not merely given back—given back with bonus and blessing. Giving, not getting, is the way. Generosity begets generosity."

Luke 6:37-38 (MSG)

My Thoughts: Letting go of your spouse's past mistakes creates an atmosphere of spiritual growth for the both of you. Bringing his or her faults and errors to his or her attention only creates chaos and strife when you're being repetitious and unkind. Keep in mind if you're always criticizing your spouse, more than likely, your spouse will find another outlet to express his or her feelings or secretly resent you. It's ok to address your views and concerns, but just be sure your heart and motive for doing so is to enhance your spouse and not tear your spouse down.

CHALLENGE: Drop that critical spirit. Instead of negatively criticizing your spouse, practice constructive criticism. I use what I call "the sandwich approach." I tell him two good things about himself before the constructive criticism, and then I tell him another good thing. This way, I start positive, stick the not so good correction in the middle, and finish off with a positive affirmation towards my spouse.

PRAYER: *Lord, please remove my need to be critical to my spouse. Help me to be kind, even in my approach to correct or express my feelings toward a negative situation. Father, help me to be honest with the disappointment of my spouse's mistake, but also keep me reminded of the fact that I have made some too. Help us both to drop the negative criticism and replace it with positive criticism.*

DAY 4

THE MAIN EVENT

"Now, getting to the questions you asked in your letter to me. First, is it a good thing to have sexual relations? Certainly—but only within a certain context. It's good for a man to have a wife, and for a woman to have a husband. Sexual drives are strong, but marriage is strong enough to contain them and provide for a balanced and fulfilling sexual life in a world of sexual disorder. The marriage bed must be a place of mutuality—the husband seeking to satisfy his wife, the wife seeking to satisfy her husband."

1 Corinthians 7:1-4 (MSG)

My Thoughts: It doesn't have to be somebody's birthday to have sex with your spouse! Many marriages are suffering in this area. God created sex for pleasure between married people. Sex with your spouse has benefits aside from being pleasurable. It has been proven to build immunity, it's also a form of exercise, it relieves stress, and it makes a person less irritable. Sex is one of the many opportunities to please your spouse and for you to be pleased also, so let's celebrate!

CHALLENGE: Have a discussion with your spouse and ask him or her if you are pleasing in the bedroom. Be willing to express your honest thoughts and brace yourself for your spouse's. Look for ways to make sex more pleasurable for the both of you!

PRAYER: *Lord, help us to be pleasing to each other in our marital bed. Teach us how to enjoy each other and to have sex frequently. Father, you created sex for our enjoyment. Help us to have eyes and a desire only for each other.*

IN THE RING

DAY 5

THE PURSE

"And if you are untrustworthy
about worldly wealth, who will trust you with the true riches of heaven?"

Luke 16:11 (TLB)

My Thoughts: Finances are very important to every household. How we govern our monies reflects our stewardship to God first and to our family. A financial vision should be created by every couple, and there must be an agreement between the two as to how that household is expected to operate. Not having that discussion or not coming into agreement will prove to be fatal in the long run.

CHALLENGE: Do you have a financial plan for your household? If so, great! But be sure to reevaluate it together and make necessary changes and adjustments. If not, set a time to meet, with all bills and expenses for the household to discuss. Create a short-term plan for the next six months to see how well it went, and then go from there. Lastly, if finances are out of control, please don't be ashamed to seek professional assistance.

PRAYER: *Father, bless the financial plan for our home. Give us the wisdom to be good stewards of what you have given us. Help us to come together as one for the benefit of* THE PURSE *in our household. Give us kingdom strategies to be successful in this area.*

DAY 6

CHOCOLATE DROP MOMENT

"I haven't spoken to my wife in years. I didn't want to interrupt her."

Rodney Dangerfield

His Thoughts: Ladies, please let us talk without you interrupting us. We have plenty we would like to express, but often, it's not heard because you're trying to interject. For a man, this is very frustrating, and it causes us to stop talking to you openly or to react in anger. We value your opinion, but sometimes, we just want to express our point of view without you commenting. We just want you to listen. Please be patient and let us get a full thought out before you say anything. Many arguments can be avoided if you use your ears more and your mouths and facial expressions less.

CHALLENGE to Wives: Practice being an active listener. Purposefully listen to understand instead of listening to respond. Be sure that your spouse is given the opportunity to finish before you cut in. Ask him about his thoughts on your communication tactics. You may be surprised as you listen with your ears and an open heart.

IN THE RING

DAY 7

CARAMEL PRINCESS NUGGETS

"Husbands, it's not just about how your wives are following; the question is how are you leading?"

~SpeakO

Her Thoughts: Sir, honestly, we don't have a problem with submitting to you. Our problem is usually about how you lead or the lack of leadership altogether. We are learning to trust you to be our head, but please don't disregard our opinions when we offer a solution for our household. Guide us lovingly, and don't forget that the Bible also says that we are to submit to one another in the fear of God. We desire to walk beside you and to follow your lead as God directs us both.

CHALLENGE to Husbands: Practice leading with love instead of dominance. Study the true definition of submission, and be willing to make changes if necessary in the way you have attempted to lead your household. Invite your wife into your studying of the word, and work together where there have been challenges.

DAY 8

PUT SOME RESPECT ON IT

"Let your conversation be always full of grace, seasoned with salt, so that you may know how to answer everyone."

Colossians 4:6 (NIV)

My Thoughts: WATCH YOUR TONE! Our tone is the true translator in every discussion. It expresses how we truly feel about the words we are speaking to our spouse, both positively or negatively. Your spouse can determine your mood during the conversation by simply listening to how your voice is being projected. Oftentimes, it's not what we say but how we say it that can cause dissention in our homes. Tone can direct conversations into an argument or into a peaceful discussion.

CHALLENGE: Be mindful of your tone when speaking to your spouse. This is not just for those heated discussions that may occur, but also for general conversations. If your spouse is telling you that your tone is disrespectful, quickly check it or pause and come back when you have made the adjustment.

PRAYER: *Father, help me to watch my words to my spouse as well as the tone that I present. Help me to speak in a way that is understandable and receptive. May my words deliver peace instead of strife as we are conversing.*

IN THE RING

DAY 9

SAVED BY THE BELL

"My feeling about in-laws was that they were outlaws."

Malcolm X

My Thoughts: I believe Malcom X either had this mindset going into his marriage or he discovered it throughout it, but one thing is for sure: he believed in boundaries. Boundaries should be created by the two of you concerning what should or should not be shared with family members and or friends. Without proper boundaries being established, small disagreements can become disastrous when added opinions begin to pile on. Disagreements, for example, between you and your spouse will be forgiven amongst the two of you, but that family member or friend will still be holding a grudge. With boundaries, these types of situations could be avoided.

CHALLENGE: Instead of picking up the phone to vent about your marital problems, be sure to pray and talk to your spouse first. Create boundaries as to what is agreed upon to be shared. Honor your spouse's wishes as best as you can. And when you have violated your agreement (hopefully this won't happen), quickly repent to your mate and do better.

PRAYER: *Father, help me to do my part in setting boundaries with my spouse. Lord, keep us both from revealing our personal business to the wrong ears. Help us to honor the boundaries we set, and if we have violated each other in this area, help us to repent quickly.*

DAY 10

THE COMBINATION

"Be completely humble and gentle; be patient, bearing with one another in love."

Ephesians 4:2

My Thoughts: On our wedding day, I'm sure we all had the thought that our spouses were perfect. Slowly, overtime, if we're honest, we all have learned differently. There are elements in every marriage that will require patience with each other. Patience is being able to discern what needs to be changed and what needs to be tolerated. Some behaviors and characteristics from your spouse will resist change, especially if you try to force it. For example, being directionally challenged or bad spending habits by your spouse may need more patience, but domestic abuse is a non-tolerable behavior. Take a step back from pushing what you think is best, and pray that God will give you more patience with your spouse. Trust me, your spouse is praying the same prayer for patience with you.

CHALLENGE: Take a moment to thank your spouse for being patient with you. Ask your spouse about areas in which he or she thinks you should have more patience. Remind them that you are in it for the long run! Remember to breathe!

PRAYER: *Dear Lord, help me to be patient with my spouse. Father, forgive me for the times I -may not have been patient, and help me in the future to not snap at my spouse in my moments of frustration. Father, let patience have her perfect work in me so that I may display that fruit more in my marriage.*

DAY 11

GO THE DISTANCE

"Don't use bad language. Say only what is good and helpful to those you are talking to, and what will give them a blessing."

Ephesians 4:29 (TLB)

My Thoughts: Stop cursing your spouse out, saints! Profane words, haughty statements, and lies are considered bad language. Many of us choose to use these types of expressions, especially when we're angry. Words have power, and once they come out, there's no taking them back. Our words have the power to put a fire out or add more fuel. Our words can hurt, or they can heal. I was once a cussing saint, and every time I was mad at my husband, cuss words would come out. I knew I needed to change, but I continued to slip up. The Holy Spirit convicted me very strongly during an argument. The soft voice said, "If your pastor was here, would you say that?" That shut my mouth right up! The same respect I would give my pastor, I needed to give my husband! I needed to learn to bless my husband and not curse him.

Challenge: Ask the Holy Spirit to convict you the moment your words are not good language. Practice the spirt of self-control, and if need be, put yourself on mute, especially when you are feeling intense. Write down scriptures about the mouth on index cards and meditate.

PRAYER: *Father, forgive me for any bad language I may have spoken out of my mouth. Help me to be a fountain of living water instead* *of a sewer with my mouth. Let my words be a blessing to my spouse and not a curse.*

IN THE RING

DAY 12

ROLL WITH THE PUNCHES

"Marriages usually include several types of rings: Engagement ring, Wedding ring, and the one most people don't want to discuss… SUFFERING!"

~SpeakO

My Thoughts: I haven't met a perfect couple or seen a marriage that didn't have its share of problems. Suffering in marriage can be a touchy subject, but one thing is for certain: we all experience it—whether it's caused by your spouse developing a serious illness, the pain of dealing with troubled kids, or, like my marriage, your union almost ending in divorce. These are examples of pain that's associated with life circumstances that might have been unexpected and sudden. I believe suffering together in these types of scenarios, is God's way of bringing us closer together as a couple. We learn to fight for each other and alongside one another. With the right focus, couples begin to build stronger marriages because of the suffering they have endured. A principle I learned during my separation with my husband was "Kintsugi." In Japanese philosophy, it treats breakage and repair of an object as beautiful rather than disguising it. In other words, what's been broken is more valued after the repair. Sufferings cause us to need repairs by a perfect God, so we must learn to embrace them because they add more value to our lives and marriages.

CHALLENGE: Evaluate your marriage and become thankful for every trial you have endured with your spouse. Invite your spouse with you down memory lane and have a praise party together. If you're newlyweds, be sure to embrace those trials together so you can celebrate down the road. Research the word Kintsugi to add more understanding as you begin to value those areas of your life that God has repaired and is repairing in your marriage.

PRAYER: *Father, help us to embrace the suffering that will and has invaded our marriage. Strengthen us both as we walk through these trials that we may come out with knowledge, wisdom, and a greater understanding. We realize that suffering will come, but we know that all things work out for our good. Help us to trust you even more as we work through our test together.*

IN THE RING

DAY 13

HITTING BELOW THE BELT

"Let us not grow weary or become discouraged in doing good, for at the proper time we will reap, if we do not give in."

Galatians 6:9 (AMP)

My Thoughts: Drop the weariness! Marriage can sometimes feel like it's taking a lot out of you spiritually, emotionally, financially, and sometimes, physically. Marital bliss seems so far away when you're battling issues and challenges in your relationship. Weariness is a sign that you are trying to change or fix things in your own strength. Replace fear with faith and trust that God will renew you day by day to hold on to His promises instead of your problem. God cares about your difficulties, and He will give you the answers you need to keep going, even when you feel like quitting.

CHALLENGE: Decide today to stop trying to fix the problems in your marriage in your own strength. Decide to believe that God will give you strength and wisdom in the face of your discouragement. Decide to praise instead of throwing pity parties.

***PRAYER**: Father, thank you that your love seeks to find me even in this dark and painful place. Please strengthen me and remove this weary spirit. Lord, allow your joy and peace to flow through me and into my marriage. Help me to hold on to your word and not give up!*

DAY 14

THE MAIN EVENT

"A good marriage isn't something you find;
it's something you make
and you have to keep on making it."
Gary Thomas

My Thoughts: Date nights are one of the ways Vincent and I make our marriage good. We schedule them regularly to ensure we are purposely spending quality time alone with each other. Date nights are a highlight for me because we take turns planning them. This allows me to step out of my norm to create an ambiance for him that involves great scenery and great food. On the other hand, his Date nights normally include an activity. Date nights don't have to be expensive, nor do they have to be done just on special occasions.

CHALLENGE: Be spontaneous and plan a date night! If you're already consistently doing that, plan something out of your norm. Instead of a restaurant, maybe go to a concert in the park. The focus is to consistently plan time for each other outside of the home environment.

PRAYER: *Father, help my spouse and me to always have a desire to date each other. Give us creative ideas on how to spruce up our date nights. Remove any stagnation in our relationship that would try to hinder us from wanting to be in each other's presence.*

IN THE RING

DAY 15

THE PURSE

"Wicked borrows and never returns; Righteous gives and gives. Generous gets it all in the end; Stingy is cut off at the pass."

Psalm 37:21 (MSG)

My Thoughts: Poor credit scores can become a source of strife in your household. Credit should have been discussed prior to marriage, but unfortunately, it is one of those subjects that can be uncomfortable to address. It can be an awkward subject to raise, but needed. Your credit score affects your household overall, so please have the discussion, even if you have prior to marriage. Do it periodically. Loan applications for houses, cars, tuition, etc. will expose each applicant, so be sure you're both in the know before an outsider has to tell you.

CHALLENGE: Be honest with your spouse concerning your individual credit scores. You credit score reflects your spending and budgeting habits. Be sure you both are working together to be financially healthy in your marriage.

PRAYER: *Father, help us to always be honest with each other concerning our finances. Give us a heart to never be ashamed or to shun each other concerning bad decisions that were made in the past. Lord, even in financial hardship, allow us to work together as a team for the betterment of our finances.*

DAY 16

Chocolate Drop Moments

"Anxiety in a man's heart weighs him down, but a good encouraging word makes it glad."

Proverbs 12:25

His Thoughts: Ladies, ladies, please compliment us more! Not only do we love and appreciate it, we need it. Throughout the course of our day, we deal with lots of criticism and just idle talking that may be going on around us. A good compliment from our wives gives us the needed encouragement to push pass the negativity. Don't just compliment us on our abilities and how we handle the kids. We want to be complimented on our looks as well! Be sincere and consistent. Your compliments encourage us to want to be better husbands to you. Don't let the ladies at the church or in the office compliment your husband more than you do. It's not that you are competing with them, but never leave that door open for the enemy to creep into your relationship because you left that door open and unattended. We want it from you, so say something nice!

CHALLENGE to Wives: Verbally compliment your spouse and let him know how much you appreciate him. Compliment how he looks in his clothing, his new haircut, or the smell of his cologne. Be sensual in your approach. Make him feel desired and wanted by you.

IN THE RING

DAY 17

CARAMEL PRINCESS NUGGETS

"Your spouse should never have to compete with anyone or anything. Honor your family members and your commitments, but put your mate FIRST!"

~SpeakO

Her Thoughts: Sir, make me feel like, no matter how busy you are, I'm first. I don't want to have to fuss to be priority or feel like I'm fighting to get your attention. Our lifelong commitment is to be present for each other, not to take each other for granted. I realize that you can't always put everything on hold for me, but make sure

I'm taken care of spiritually, physically, and emotionally before you get burned out with family members, kids, work, ministry, etc. No one else can fill the void I experience when you ignore me, whether it's intentional or not. I want your attention, and I want to give you mine.

CHALLENGE to Husband: Text her and/or call her frequently just to check on her and let her know you love her. Clear your schedule and take her out consistently. Tell the fellas, "not this time, I'm going to watch the game with 'wifey.'" Ask her about some of the things you do or have done in the past that make her feel like she's number one in your life. The focus is being consistent with how she feels and accommodating as best as you can.

DAY 18

PUT SOME RESPECT ON IT

"And to esteem them very highly in love because of their work. Be at peace among yourselves."

I Thessalonians 5:13 (RSV)

My Thoughts: Speaking well of your spouse in public is one of the most powerful ways you can show respect. It is an awesome display of how you feel and what is expected from others concerning how they should treat your spouse as well. It's even a better feeling for your spouse when they catch you doing it. It validates your spouse and even boosts his or her self-confidence. Observers pick up or catch on to how you both feel about each other by what you demonstrate. Be careful to keep in mind that even when your spouse may have upset you, the public doesn't need to know about it.

CHALLENGE: Be intentional with giving your spouse praise and honor in public. Find different avenues to display your respect for your spouse. Events, public settings, social media, or family gatherings are all different opportunities to say something nice about your mate. I'm sure your spouse wouldn't mind some extra public praise.

PRAYER: *Father, help us both to be mindful of how we speak to one another, but also about each other. Help us to be intentional about praising our spouse in public. Show us how to mirror the respect that we have for each other to encourage observers to be respectful to our mate as well. Lord, even when we may not agree with each other, help us remain respectful.*

IN THE RING

DAY 19

SAVED BY THE BELL

"Train up a child in the way he should go, and when he is old he will not depart from it."

Proverbs 22:6

My Thoughts: Parents, as much as possible, be on the same page with the disciplines and raising of the children that are in your household. I say this very gently because there are those who may have blended families such as myself, and many times, the unity wasn't displayed between my spouse and me, which was likely confusing to the children. Be sure that the rules that are set are agreed upon between the two of you before presenting them. Be considerate of the fact that your spouse may or may not have come from the same type of background and that you two won't always agree on the "how's" to handle "the situation." Parenting can be both enjoyable and stressful, but have each other's back during the process. Just remember to do your best together to show them God's way, which will include His word.

CHALLENGE: Try very hard not to argue in front of the children, especially while disciplining them. Listen to each other's ideas as to how to handle situations that may arise. Discuss your rearing styles, and try to incorporate what worked well for your parents when they were raising you. If one of your ideas didn't work, go back to the drawing board together.

PRAYER: *Father, bless our family and give us as parents the wisdom we need to rear our children. Teach us how to raise righteous, God-fearing children that will follow our example of the word of God. Teach us how to be the best parents we can be to our children. Show us how to parent your way*

IN THE RING

-DAY 20

THE COMBINATION

"Be kind and helpful to one another, tender-hearted [compassionate, understanding], forgiving one another [readily and freely], just as God in Christ also forgave you."

Ephesians 4:32 (MSG)

My Thoughts: Forgiveness is one of the most necessary ingredients to have a successful marriage. Most of my problem with forgiveness was that I didn't know what it really meant to let go of the hurt that was caused, nor did I know how to move past me hurting my spouse. Forgiveness is a dual blessing in your relationship. It frees both the one that caused the offense, and it frees you to still be able to love and nurture your spouse despite the hurt it may have caused. Most of us know that forgiveness is required, but it's still hard for us to do. Here are a few tips that blessed our marriage.

- Forgiveness is not letting our spouse off the hook. We can, and should, still hold our spouse accountable for his or her actions or lack of actions when offense takes place. This opens the door for us to try to understand each other's perspective and be willing to adjust so that same hurt won't occur again.
- Forgiveness does not mean denying reality or ignoring the hurt that has taken place. Forgiveness helps you both accept what has happened, but grants your spouse the open invitation to follow up with a change in his or her actions.

- Forgiveness is deciding that we won't allow negative feelings to dictate how we treat each other. Always make the extra effort to draw closer to your spouse.
- Forgiveness is a process, not an event. It might take some time to work through your emotional attachment to the hurt before you can truly forgive, but be willing to still love and nurture your marriage in the process of healing.
- Forgiveness starts with a mental decision. It starts with a willingness to be obedient to the Word of God.

CHALLENGE: Reread the strategies on forgiveness and execute them.

PRAYER: *Father, help us to forgive each other quickly without holding grudges. Cleanse our hearts from any old offenses that we may have carried, and give us the needed strength to let it go. Help us to be more sensitive to each other's feelings, and help our marriage to be healed.*

IN THE RING

DAY 21

GO THE DISTANCE

"Keep your mouth closed and you'll stay out of trouble."

Proverbs 21:23 (TLB)

My Thoughts: Silence, in many situations in your marriage, can be a blessing. Keeping your mouth closed can minimize the chances of you saying the wrong thing or saying something you will regret later. Silence offers you an opportunity to make a sound judgment, process your emotions, and digest what has been spoken to you. Silence, especially in the face of chaos in your marriage, benefits your stress levels and adds character to your spiritual development. The quote, "Silence is golden," simply means saying nothing is preferable than speaking in many circumstances. Be aware that the attitude behind your silence is just as valuable as the silence itself. Remember, God looks at the inward attitudes as well as the words that come out of our mouth.

CHALLENGE: Practice being quiet during disagreements with your spouse. Be sure to explain to your mate that you are processing what he or she is saying and how you are feeling. The goal here is not to give your spouse the "silent treatment," but to help him or her understand you may simply need to cool off before responding. Also, this silence allows you to check your attitude and how you're feeling within so that when you do respond, it won't be with regret.

PRAYER: *Father, help us to practice silence in our marriage at the appropriate time. Help us both to be mindful that words have power and we desire to use our words effectively towards each other. Lord, let our words bring us closer together and not push us further apart. Father, keep us mindful during our silence to check our inner attitude.*

IN THE RING

DAY 22

ROLL WITH THE PUNCHES

"Submit to one another out of reverence for Christ. Wives submit yourselves to your own husband as you do to the Lord. For the husband is the head of the wife as Christ is the head of the church, his body, of which he is the Savior. Now as the church submits to Christ, so also wives should submit to their husbands in everything."

Ephesians 5:21-24

My Thoughts: Although submission has become a dirty word for some, now that I have understanding, it is a blessing. Submission is NOT associated with being docile, weak, or degrading, but on the contrary, it is a sign of strength and obedience to the word of God. Having a mutual respect in your marriage will be key to submitting. Recognize that God had both parties in mind when he put the man as the head of the household. You, wife, are his support system and not his servant in your marriage. This brought a sense of peace in this area for me. As a couple, we must learn to work together and respect the order that God has set by not resisting it. Submission is coming under the power and authority of another willingly. It doesn't mean that one party dominates, but that both partners are focused on loving, supporting, and helping their mate.

CHALLENGE: Study the biblical definition of submission. If there is a struggle, be sure to ask God to give you a heart to obey his word. Have a conversation with your spouse as to why this may or may not bother you. Find tangible ways to submit to your mate. Practice putting each other's needs first.

PRAYER: *Father, give us both a heart to submit to you and to one another. Give us wisdom in this area as we strive to obey your word. Show us, Lord, how to be submissive to each other and to do it willingly without force. Let your will be done in this area of submission.*

IN THE RING

DAY 23

HITTING BELOW THE BELT

"Comparison is the root cause of all evil. Why compare when no two people are alike?"

Haresh Sippy

My Thoughts: Comparing your spouse to someone else's is a recipe for disaster. It will breed strife. Those comparisons will blind you to the gifts and talents that God has given your spouse to be a blessing to your marriage. It also fuels resentment towards you from your spouse if he or she is aware you are comparing him or her. Any time there are comparisons, the words "either" or "other" are used to distinguish our perception. This is not a pleasant view when we're trying to match our spouse up with someone else's because that could mean we prefer that person's spouse over our own. Unlike many of my friends, my husband is not a preacher, but he is awesome at building things with his hands and supporting my ministry behind the scenes. Learn to appreciate who and what your partner provides to you and for you. This helps us to have a spirit of gratitude verses a critical one.

CHALLENGE: Intentionally focus on the areas that you love about your spouse. If there are areas in which you desire to see change in your spouse, then have that discussion, but be willing to receive feedback on your spouse's desired changes for you. The goal is always to build each other up and show gratitude for each other.

PRAYER: *Father, help us to accept one another and to be grateful for each other's qualities. Please remove any comparisons towards our spouse from our hearts and minds. Show us both how to appreciate one another, and if there are ways we can become better towards each other to enhance our marriage, give us a heart to work on them together.*

IN THE RING

DAY 24

THE MAIN EVENT

"No matter how old you both get, never stop holding hands, never stop dancing, and never stop saying I love you."

Author Unknown

My Thoughts: PDA (Public Display of Affection) is one of our favorite past times. We happen to be an affectionate couple in and out of the public eye. PDA can range from kisses, touches, words, and/or the wink of the eye to your spouse. It doesn't have to have heavy sexual under tones that leave others uncomfortable and appear as if you're trying to prove that you love each other.

It's simply giving your spouse that extra intimacy that connects you in your relationship. PDA touches can be calming for your spouse. They also show that your presence is present in that moment with him or her, and hopefully it leads to a "FIRE" in your bedroom! Some relationships have become stale and boring due to a lack of PDA because the playfulness with each other has been avoided and diminished. Our children often say, "UGGHHH!" when they see us exchanging PDA, but they are also smiling because they see the love we have for each other.

CHALLENGE: If PDA is missing from your marriage, you initiate it! Take it slow and subtle, especially if it hasn't always been a part of your relationship. If PDA had once been a part of your relationship but you guys may have lost your way, then definitely take a trip together down memory lane and catch up! Create ways to show your spouse that you are still attracted to him or her, and let the playfulness begin! Rub your spouse's back, hold your spouse's hand, whisper in your spouse's ear, sneak a kiss on his or her neck, whatever it takes to be frisky with your spouse!

PRAYER: *Father, thank You for our marriage. I pray that our relationship continues to grow and mature as you have purposed it. Father, let us become more and more affectionate towards each other and our love for each other will be displayed wherever we are. Help us to always be appropriate in our PDA and considerate to those who may be around. Seal our marriage with love and compassion for each other as we are intentional about the intimacy in our relationship.*

IN THE RING

DAY 25

THE PURSE

"Couples who want unity in marriage need to be willing to depend on each other for accountability and support, especially in finances. The goal is to come from what's mine is mine to what's OURS is OURS!"

~SpeakO

My Thoughts: Numerous studies have proven that arguing over finances is at the top of the list for reasons couples fight. Most of that stems from the "me" and "my" mindset that has not been dealt with before the nuptials. Talking finance is not an easy subject but is necessary to enhance the oneness that you should pursue for your marriage. Decisions for your household should be made together, and the power of agreement is necessary. Merging together in your finances helps you become stronger as a couple. You learn to depend, support, and become accountable to each other to accomplish the goals that you set for your home.

CHALLENGE: Be open and willing to work together with your spouse concerning your household finances. Get rid of the "MY/MINE" MINDSET. Decide to stop keeping secrets from each other in this area. The goal is not to micromanage each other, but to be open and willing to agree with how the household is affected by our decisions. Every decision that is made in agreement with each other brings your marriage closer to unity.

PRAYER: *Father, create in us a clean heart, and renew in us a right spirit concerning the financial state of our marriage. Help us both to* *be open and honest with each other in this area so that the enemy will have no foothold in causing division. Lord, by faith we are standing strong in our finances, and through your grace, we will continue to build a strong financial foundation for our household.*

IN THE RING

DAY 26

CHOCOLATE DROP MOMENT

"Husbands want sex more than just on our birthdays, holidays, and special occasions. We want 'due benevolence'!"

Vincent Speakman Sr.

His Thoughts: Ladies, as your husbands, we want you to know that we want more sex. We want "due benevolence." This is what I say to my wife as a playful code between us. As men, we desire sex with you—period. We don't like when you use it as a form of manipulation against us, nor do we agree when sex is withheld because you're mad. The truth of matter is that we still desire you even when you are mad at us, and most of us believe that sex will relieve some of the stress so we can communicate better together after an argument. Ladies, we want you to initiate sex with us sometimes as well. We crave your kisses and touches. Surprise us at the door by wearing some high heels, your best-smelling perfume, and NOTHING else. These random acts boost our egos and makes us desire you even more!

CHALLENGE: Go to a lingerie store and pick out some pieces that will excite your husband. Pick a random night, prepare his favorite meal, and let the games begin. Sext him (send him a text with a little dirty talk) to arouse him and show him you desire him as well.

DAY 27

CARAMEL PRINCESS MOMENTS

"Match Her Effort.

Respect Her Hustle.

Support Her Ambition.

Protect her Heart.

Value Her Loyalty.

Uplift Her Spirit. Love Her Unconditionally."

Author Unknown

My Thoughts: I was sent this quote in my social media inbox from a wife that was in ministry and was hurting due to a lack of support from her spouse who was not in ministry. I knew this feeling because I have been in her shoes. Sir, we want you to support us. We want you to be present in every area of lives, even when you may not be familiar with that territory. Be a sounding board for us, be our biggest fan, lift us up when we seem down in our spirit, and encourage us by reminding us that we can accomplish any goal we set our minds to. As your wife, we want you to match our efforts. Many times, society has made us feel that we should follow behind you and support your dreams and visions as if we shouldn't have our own. Trust me—we do have them, and our hope is that, ultimately, they will correspond with yours to make our household greater. We need your protection, your support, your loyalty, and unconditional love as your partner to be all that God has called us to as well.

CHALLENGE: Husbands, show up at her ministry or business event and cheer her on. Listen to her talk about her dream and goals; then find ways to let her know you were listening. Invest monetarily into her projects if you are able, and volunteer to help wherever she needs it. For example, my husband will often drive me to ministry events and serve at my book table. Other times when I come home from a speaking event, he may have dinner prepared and a nice foot rub on the agenda. The goal is to let her know you are proud of her and supporting her.

DAY 28

PUT SOME RESPECT ON IT

"Proverbs 31 Priority List:

GOD = *Your personal relationship with Him*

SPOUSE = *Your First Priority after God*

Family = *Children, other family members, friends, associates*

Ministry = *Activities for church, speaking engagements, book writing's, etc.*

I had to learn to make my husband 'The Priority,' not just an option!"

~SpeakO

MY THOUGHTS: When my marriage fell apart and divorce was on the table, I blamed my husband for everything! In my mind, it was all his fault because I was walking in the call of God for my life, or so I thought. It wasn't until God showed me that my affair or my "side piece" was with ministry! My priorities were out of order and caused me to neglect my spouse. I had chosen writing books, preaching on platforms, and being on many prayer lines over spending quality time with my husband. I had neglected him but gave attention to everything else that I thought made me happy. I had become a public success but a private failure, and this is when God revealed His order for my household to me in a very personal way. My maturity increased when I was able to see and own my error. God began to restore our broken pieces when I got my priorities aligned with His word!

CHALLENGE: Take a closer look at what you give most of your attention to and ask yourself, "Are my priorities in alignment with God's Word? Have my priorities been fair to my spouse?" Make the adjustments. The goal is not to keep you from enjoying other activities, but to be sure your spouse feels like the priority in your life instead of an option.

PRAYER: *Father, open our eyes and hearts that we may learn to honor our spouses as the priority in our lives. Teach us how to make each other secure in our relationship. Guide us in how we prioritize our schedules, and show us how to make the most of our time together. If we have been out of order in this area, help us to repent to you and to each other.*

DAY 29

SAVED BY THE BELL

"Family Traditions help create lasting memories. Family Traditions are made to impart value into our children, a sense of identity. Family Traditions are created to give those we love a sense of belonging and offer them a security that the outside world can't penetrate. Be sure your Family Traditions reflect what you both would love to see duplicated throughout future generations."

~SpeakO

MY THOUGHTS: Family traditions reflect the values that have prevailed throughout generations. They are the principles and creative flow of how your family operates as it tends to change and grow overtime. Family traditions are constant efforts to create memorable moments with those you treasure the most. I remember enjoying "FRIDAY NIGHT WRESTLING" as a child where we ate all kinds of junk food and sat in front of the TV with our dad. Of course, we watched some of the wrestling program, but it was mostly laughter and conversation that took place in those moments. Family dinners and gatherings give us the opportunity to catch up on what's going on with each other, they allow us to share our hearts with one another, and they provided a place to even get good advice for what may have been troubling us. My household has adopted some of those ideas, and we're hoping our children will for their families as well.

CHALLENGE: Think about the family traditions that have added value to your life over the years and consider implementing them in your household. Begin to create new ways to bond your family together that you and your spouse agree on. It may be something simple like "Movie Night" or family dinners on a specific day and time. Remember, for it to be a tradition, it must be consistent!

PRAYER: *Father, give my spouse and me ideas on how to bring our family closer. Help us to honor those traditions that have helped us to be productive in our lives. Father, we desire to teach our family values that can be passed down to future generations, so give us a heart to create family traditions that are healthy and nurturing for our spirits and our souls.*

DAY 30

THE COMBINATION

"A marriage where you can pray, worship, and passionately pursue the will of GOD together is so worth fighting for! Most of our battles are fought in prayer. Praying together makes the fight easier!"

~SpeakO

MY THOUGHTS: When asking a few married couples a question concerning prayer, initially, I was shocked to discover that many of them didn't pray together. Both spouses stated they prayed *for* each other, but they did not actually pray together other than before meals. Honestly, I was conducting the survey because my husband and I weren't praying together either. It had never really occurred to us that we needed to until I was reading the Word at a very difficult time in our marriage, and this scripture jumped out at me. Matthew 18:19 spoke to my heart concerning two agreeing on earth and how it would be done by our heavenly Father! That word encouraged us to pray together every morning before either of us leave the house. We recognized that, in our greatest fight, praying together caused us to be naked in the spirit (uncovered, exposed to each other's thoughts and feelings). This understanding alone helped us to recognize that, together, we are becoming stronger against the enemy attacks, but more vulnerable to each other in the presence of our God. We believe praying together as a couple drew us closer to God and to each other.

CHALLENGE: Choose a place and time to pray together consistently. Hold hands as you pray, and keep your sessions short. It may feel awkward at first, but the more you pray together, the easier it becomes. Keep in mind, this is the person you go to bed with, the person you wake up to. You know his or her weaknesses and strengths, and he or she knows yours. This is the closest person to you, and prayer will bring you both closer to each *other and God.*

PRAYER: *Father, as we present ourselves to you in prayer together, please strengthen us as a couple. Allow your spirit to guide every word out of our mouths concerning our family, decisions, and struggles we may be facing. Bring us into a place of peace with you and with each other. Teach us how to fight together in the spirit, and cover us from any and every attack of the enemy. Open our hearts. Infuse us with love, joy, and peace for this* *day. Help us to grow closer to you as we also seek to be closer to each other.*

DAY 31

THE MAIN EVENT

"Stay on good terms with each other, held together by love. Be ready with a meal or a bed when it's needed. Why, some have extended hospitality to angels without ever knowing it! Regard prisoners as if you were in prison with them. Look on victims of abuse as if what happened to them had happened to you. Honor marriage and guard the sacredness of sexual intimacy between wife and husband. God draws a firm line against casual and illicit sex."

Hebrews 13:4 (MSG)

MY THOUGHTS: The Bible makes it clear that marriage is honorable and that the bed is UNDEFILED! That means that any type of sex I share with my spouse and any way my spouse and I decide to share it with each other is permissible. The subject of oral sex, for many years, has had the Christian community on the fence as people always ask, "is that ok with God?" I have not found oral sex in any bible translation as prohibited, unnatural, unhealthy, harmful, or unkind. As a matter of fact, it's quite the opposite: enjoyable, pleasurable, and loving if the both of you agree. Of course, sexual pleasures should not be forced upon your spouse, nor should either one of you feel pressured if you're uncomfortable. God created sex for the enjoyment of married couples, and the focus should be on you both pleasing each other. In a biblically beautiful marriage, we have the right to enjoy each other, so let the celebrations begin, even if it's not either one of your birthdays!

CHALLENGE: Play a question/answer game with your spouse to see how he or she really feels about oral sex. Does your spouse like it? Why or why not? Are there other sexual favors your spouse desires but hasn't shared? Each of you should write down your honest answer and allow your spouse to read it out loud. Hopefully, you both can walk away with clarity and are comfortable after you have discussed this. Now, it's time to CELEBRATE!

ABOUT THE AUTHOR

Orienthia Renee Speakman is tagged by many as "The Keep it Real Preacher!" Her energetic and transparent messages have touched the hearts of individuals, both near and abroad. Her ability to take biblical principles and teach others how to use them in a practical way has been what has drawn much attention to her in recent years.

Orienthia has been ordained in ministry since October 2000. She has effectively served in various capacities as her heart is to operate with excellence in whatever role she plays. A college graduate with a BS in Psychology, she currently serves her local church as the Christian Education Pastor. Orienthia's love for education has her in pursuit of ultimately earning a Doctorate in Ministry.

Orienthia can minister on many topics, but her heart is for helping others to renew, rebuild, and reinvent themselves after tragedy. Orienthia often says, "Every individual has the right to have a strong comeback from any setback in their lives. There is power in their process, and my goal is to help them to be committed to their RESILIENCE!"

Her ministry and business, Speak O Worldwide, houses a variety of resources to nurture broken individuals into wholeness. Her Butterfly boot camp was created specifically for the needs of women who have been divorced, widowed, or are just making bad choices in relationships and desire to be healed. It is a nine-week course that can be done from home via telephone or internet. Her coaching services, books and other materials can also be found on her website.

Orienthia loves speaking, writing, and being a Transformation Coach, but her priority is her marriage! Her book, *"Marriage Vs. Ministry, The Fight of My Life"* is a candid, uncensored tool to share the dangers of an improper balance between the two. She and her husband, Vincent, were almost another statistic for divorce but used the principles in this book to not only save their marriage, but to have a healthy one. This couple shares five beautiful children and resides in Stone Mountain, Georgia.

Contact Information :
www.speakorienthia.com
Fb Contacts: Orienthia Speakman
Speak O
Butterfly University
IG Contact: pastorospeaks

Made in the USA
Middletown, DE
15 March 2022

62681368R00071